Why Side Chicks Winning?

By

Shanti Helena

ISBN: 978-0-692-06557-0 (sc)
Editors: P31 Publishing, LLC
For more information, please visit www.shantihelena.com
Instagram: shanti.helena

Holy Bible, New International version, NIV, Copyright 1973, 1978, 1984, 2011 by Biblica, Inc. Used by permission. All rights reserved.

Because of the dynamic nature of the Internet, any web addresses or links contained in this book may have changed since publication and may no longer be valid. The views expressed in this work are solely those of the author and do not necessarily reflect the views of the publisher, and the publisher disclaims any responsibility for them.

Any people depicted in stock imagery are models, and such images are being used for

Illustrative purposes only. Shanti Helena 2/21/2018

Dedication

This is dedicated to all the women who have been cheated on...side chick or main chick. No one's love life is perfect, but it can be satisfying. I've had my heart broken in quite a few monogamous relationships. I thought I was a good main woman. However, there was a better side chick waiting in the wings. I was also a side chick in my last relationship- and baby, I was winning! I will share that story later. That journey taught me a great deal about expectations and desires between men and women. So, I took the cumulative experience, which evolved into the book "Why Side Chicks Winning?". Hopefully I can share with you on how to keep your man exempt from side chicks.

I want you to be open-minded to both sides of the equation. Place yourself in the other woman's shoes. Look at relationship needs and desires through the eyes of both main and side chick. You just might learn a thing or two on how to step up your game.

It is my sincere hope that this book will help you better your relationship by take a glimpse into and few lessons from the world of side chicks.

Table of Contents

CHAPTER 1

The Different Type of Side Chicks

Y ou need to face some real shit right here, right now. Self-evaluate baby. Are you a side chick and just don't know it? Just don't want to face it? Want to hide from the possibility? Guess what- suck it up and accept the signs…the damn facts! Wondering where I'm going with this topic? Recognize sister! Are you feeling any of the vibes from the types listed below?

Side Chick 1 - Clueless

This chick is completely unaware (in the beginning) to her current situation. She's happy with him. They met, things were smooth. Hmmm, this could be the one. She was in a bad space, tired of running through all the bullshit men that come with the search for the right one. In other words, her head and heart were in a bad mental space. She was weary from wanting the love of a good man.

Understand, this is not your average side chick, the 'I know I'm your side chick' woman. He doesn't hide her from the public. He introduces her to his friends. He stays overnight sometimes 3 to 4 times in a week! So she says to herself, "He can't have another woman….let alone a wife with children and mother-in-law, etc." The sex is AMEN-ZING!!!!! In other words…his love making is close to heaven on earth as you can imagine. He does all the close, intimate things to find his way to your heart….at least for a good six months straight. During that time she never suspects, she only

1

trusts in him. She thinks, "Why would I snoop around through his phone or social media accounts… that man is good to me! Damn, he even involves me in his entrepreneurial endeavors!"

He is so open with her. He shares his hopes and visions for the future. He describes his fears and apprehensions. He opens his life book up to her. And she falls right on in. She decides, "I'm gonna help him make it happen for us!"

Oops, there it is. She put it all on the line…her vajaja has his name written all on it. He knows her credit score, her income, and her ability to make shit happen. Now she's fucked! Now she is loving in the blind. Beware! Men can sense when a woman is weak and unaware and will take advantage. In this scenario, it comes in the 7th month.

Let us talk about this unaware side chick for a moment. Her main attribute is that she is focused on HIM. She is focused on what she can do for THEM. To her fault, she did not do her due diligence. After all, he pays rent and lives with her. She didn't snoop or investigate his back story.

Side chick is on point to getting that man…your man. She is on the road to winning. Obviously, something is wrong in your camp. The question to the main chick is, how and why does he have time for her? She's not stalking him; he came in search of her. In search of something missing from you. She opened her door with kindness on one of the many nights you and he got into it.

This side chick THINKS he's her man. She doesn't know about you. Why? Why fault her? She's in the blind. You are mad because she has the pedal to the metal for who she thinks is her man. You once did. They're video chatting, sending cute texts and pics and being spontaneous, and grabbing nights out on the town. When he comes to her bed, it smells sweet. She looks sexy. She is sexy in the way he wants their sex to be. What's going on in your bedroom?

The words that roll from her tongue encourage, inspire and bring in a whirlwind of hope for the future, the possibilities of winning in life. So, he spends his most valuable assets, his time and his money, with her. This chick is playing to win. She just might.

Take a page from her book: Look the part. Like Nike....Just Do It! Listen to him. Communicate. Cook. Clean. Turn the game on. Run a hot shower/bath. Pour the wine. Give him a hot oil massage in your sexy clothes. Give him "top" while watching TV. Sex it out in unusual areas in the house.

You need to find the good for "US" again with your man. Bitching ain't it. Talk, listen, and remember when it was about "US". Go back to the drawing board. If it's worth it, do it. Learn to disagree without being disagreeable.

She is not stunting him at all! She has her own career, own money, own crib, own personal life, sense of humor, and good credit. And she is bringing it all to the table. Bring it all to him. There will be a very good chance he'll never leave the side chick alone completely. You want his mind to be at standstill when it's time to choose between the both of you. He has to think about your history. You never left him when he treated your life badly. You may have kids together. Make him know the side chick is not worth losing you.

Ladies, corner his mind frame today! Start making changes. It may sound hard, but is he worth it to you? Think of your relationship as an actual product that you're trying to sell to a customer. When you want to close the deal on the sale, you eventually have the customer in a position where their appetite hollers "I must have that". Create a need and want for the "US" you both had/have. Give him his own personalized "side chick" in you. Think of it this way, you're trying to satisfy those "ragging cravings" he wants from the side chick. Once he's given in, you're good to go. Just maintain baby!

Consistency is the key. Keep him on his toes. Sexual excitement mixed with a shot of unpredictability is a good thing. Looking good matters. Men are visual and need attention and validation. I want you to win him back and keep him!

Please do NOT fight for him if he's not worth it. Check your rationale. What does he bring to your life? I know we are in a competitive world. Ladies, DO NOT compete for the sake of only winning. Is he a prize? Is he worth it? I remember I was always after guys that all the women wanted. I did that just to win. The sad part is once I got him, he wasn't what I needed or wanted.

Before you go to battle against the encroaching side chick, be ready for the fight and be sure, very sure, he's worth it.

Short Story:

I'm going to share a little story with you. I know a woman who was with her man for over 10 years. They were comfortable with each other. When he first met her, she was his shining star. They became that ride-or- die couple. They traveled the world together. They had two kids and eventually got married. His lifestyle had a twist to it. He was a regular businessman, but a street guy also (if you know what I mean, lol). She's well educated and on the cute side, extremely motivated and confident. Three years into the "marriage", things changed. It became mundane. He went to work. She went to work. They met up at home. She cooked and helped the children with homework. He stepped out to take care of "other" businesses. They went to bed and started the routine over again each day.

Less and less time was dedicated to them as a couple. She became 90 percent devoted to motherhood. The balance of her time was divided between friends and extended family members. She began to lose her sexy.

He became more married to getting money. In search of it, he spent more time away from home and in the streets with his friends. All of his friends had side chicks too.

ATTENTION: Watch the company your man keeps. He may not be like them at first, but certain traits will rub off on him.

Ultimately, their relationship slip began to slide into minimal communication. This was the perfect opportunity for a side chick. Unfortunately for their marriage, he met a side chick, type 1.

His boo thang had her own money, good credit, own crib, own car and her sexy was on fleek!

When they first met, there was no intention of a full- bloom romance. Due to the fact that there was zero communication at home, more likely a thing would develop between the two. Over drinks, they talked about their financial aspirations. Over numerous dinners they discussed their career goals, their beliefs, and their dreams. Then one day she invited him over.

The house was super clean, smelling good and well decorated. He was very impressed. During all the discussions between them, he never once mentioned his family. This woman piqued his interest. So he kept that dirty little secret to himself. He began coming over for dinner, lunch, movies, football, basketball and sex snacks. The sex was all he and she both desired. Needless to say, he became MIA at home.

This went on for 8 months before the SH*# hit the fan. He fell in love with this clueless woman. She fell in love with him. He was faced with a dilemma. He didn't want to lose his children. He didn't want to lose his new found love. So, he came clean- in a little dirty way. He LIED. He told her he was in the midst of a divorce. Of course, she was angry but she forgave him and did the "oh I'll stand by my man thing". In her case, it was a good decision. She stood and he stood with her. Within the next year, he was divorced and living with the woman- I'll call her clueless side chick 1.

If there is a moral here, it is most definitely for the wife. Remember to nourish your relationship with your husband with the same intensity as you did in the beginning. In these days and times, maybe even more.

Side Chick 2 - The Aware Chick

Oh baby…She is very aware of her role. She is the freaky, fun, open- minded, sexy, beautiful to her damn self, high confidence and high maintenance chick…..with options!

This chick does not care about you at all. She just wants to have fun, get money, and have sex. Men know that if you have one of these, you are not the only one and it's a 50/50 chance he can make her his own. You have to come with it and come correct with this side chick!

Side Chick 2 provides that edgy lifestyle most men yearn for. That age-old adage that the forbidden fruit is the sweetest, is his new relationship experience. The thrill of the chase and the excitement of his hidden secret keeps his ego totally satisfied.

There is fun outside the bedroom too. She brings spontaneity to his world. For example, she'll text him and invite him to watch dirty movies and hard porn together (sometimes in the middle of a work day). She takes him to the football game. She cheers rigorously with him. This chick exploits his interests. She specializes in keeping excitement in the game. She turns him out sexually. They would have sex anywhere from the club to the damn movies!

As long as this side chick is interested in him, she'll attentively listen to his life's plights. Occasionally, she'll see where she can bring ease to his situations. She is drama free. She is a nice slice of easy cake. Side Chick 2 finds his sexuality is his weak spot.

Take notes from her ladies! Be like her! Be his sex slave sometimes! Go to the sex store and buy a few items. Observe his reactions in the bedroom. I bet he'll be thinking *What in the hell is this...I love it!* Incorporate this in your sexual routine. I suggest not more than twice or three times a week.

If your man is already caught up with this type of chick, you better drop the mundane and bust out with some sexy tricks on his ass. ALL of the men I interviewed for this book said they love it when a woman dresses a little slutty. They want a strong sex appeal type of woman. Next time you go shopping, grab that shirt that enhance/exposes your breasts. When you two go on a date night, wear that short fitted red dress with your Ruby Woo matte lipstick. Size doesn't matter either ladies. Men love BBW to petite women. Turn the heads of men and women when you walk in the club or the restaurant. Let me tell you a little secret. Men like it when their woman gets attention from both genders!

I want you to create a sexual plan for your man. Do a 30 to 90-day freak challenge for him. It will become a habit. Go shopping for sexy clothes. No more conservative, grandma wear around him! Please do not wear Tammy Roman's hair wrap either! Turn up your savage today!

Side Chick 3 - A Combo

Well, well, well, look what we have here ladies, a combo side chick! This side chick is very tricky. This side chick has a combination of both side chick number 1 and 2. SMH! What are you going to do? You have a lot to deal with now. At this point of their relationship, they're both in too deep. They have been dating for years. She knows the truth. She has become OK with being with him, even after knowing! After all, he pays her rent, showers her with gifts, gives her lots of attention, and much more!

Did you honestly think it would be easy for her to walk away from him? HELL NO! Please don't be mad at her because she was unaware of the wife for a very long time. Feelings and emotions are involved super heavy on both sides!

Situation 1 - Main Chick/Side Chick

This side chick has so many mixed emotions about what to do next. She is so in love with him, but he has a main woman. It's a very hard situation to handle. He is her king and she is his queen. He stays with the main, because, face it.....it's cheaper to keep her.

The side chick actually left him alone after the blow up about the main woman. Guess who came back for her months after she left? Ding dong, your MAN! Girl, what are you doing wrong? You were given the chance to be the woman he wanted and your ass failed! Can you win him back? It's going to be very hard. You have three options to handle this situation. First, you can GET YOUR SHIT TOGETHER and be like "her". Do this ONLY IF HE'S WORTH IT. Secondly, you can accept who he is and deal with the fact that he will always mess with her. Lastly, you can leave his ass alone. The ball is in your court. I cannot tell you what to do. I can give you options to choose from. I'm sure you're thinking, "I'm winning because he's still here with me." So fucking what that he is still with you? This Side Chick is still winning because he never left her alone to begin with! He's still not totally yours the way you want. Change the game up on his ass- today!

Situation 2: Wife/Side Chick

Well, let's say she met him unexpectedly. They started dating and things got real with them. After 7 to 8 months of dating, it was rumored that he was married. She questioned him about the situation. Of course, his ass lied to the Side Chick.

She saw him earlier on that day when it all went down! They were chilling and cuddling at her house. Later that night, she received a very disturbing call about him from his own best friend!

Side Chick: "Hey honey, I heard some real bad news about you today. Please tell me it's not true!" (She's screaming and crying.)

Him: "Baby, calm down. What's wrong?"

Side Chick: "Are you fucking married?"

Him: "Who told you that lie? Hell no! No! I'm not married! Who told you that damn lie?"

Side Chick: "Your best friend!"

He ended up fighting so hard till he won her back. He did win her back. However, he continued lying about his marital status. He stayed on point with her for a while. She ended up believing him because he never gave her any signs of being married or with another woman. A few months passed and they are happy love birds AGAIN. She had a few pregnancy scares in between the time. He conveyed to her how wonderful it would be to have "their" child. At this point she did not care if she got pregnant. In her mind, their relationship is unbreakable.

Well, what's done in the dark does come to the light.

It was around his birthday when shit got real. They had plans to go to Tampa, FL with mutual friends. She had just graduated with her Masters. She had intentions of celebrating his birthday and her academic accomplishment. She canceled due to a squabble with a friend. While he was out of town, they were talking and texting heavily. She ended up going out with her friends that same weekend to celebrate in Chicago. She sent him lots of sexy pictures and messages the entire weekend. Now typically, when he goes out of town, he comes to her house from the airport. She was anxiously waiting on him that Sunday night. All that day she was also experiencing a gut feeling that something bad was about to happen. His texts began to slack up till eventually there were none and no responses, as Sunday was approaching.

Ladies, pay attention to intuition.

She continued to call and text on Monday; another woman was not even on her radar at the time. She was nervous over the fact that something might have happened to him. Two days later, she received a 3- way call from his best friend AGAIN. She was informed that he was indeed married and the wife found out about everything. The wife had text messages and pictures to prove her husband was living a double life. This Side Chick was so hurt and was lost for words.

During that time, he worked near her apartment. He was a construction worker for a very large company in Chicago. She had thought of showing up at his job and going crazy. However, she just wasn't that type of woman to do something like that anyway. She blew his phone up with calls and texts all week long. He still did not respond to her with anything! He eventually blocked her from calling. At that point, she said fuck it and walked away. Three months later, he finally came around and admitted his marital status and mixed it with a little lie. He was supposedly legally separated and was over his marriage all together.

Well, his come-back was strong enough for her at the time. He wasn't happy in the marriage prior to her. He was legally separated, and he loved her so much, blah, blah, blah. Let's not forget he showered her with gifts and lots of money too!

The Side chick took him back. She told him honestly what she was expecting from him moving forward from that point. Now, both main and side chick are aware of each other at this point. They both frantically dig into all social media to learn what they can learn about each other. See, the side chick had a strong hold on him to the point that he was about to leave his family. However, it's cheaper to keep her (the wife).

He was highly aware of her expectations from him moving forward (during the divorce process) and he respected that too. You know he gave her this "I Have a Dream" speech on his love for her. Yes, ladies this guy was very good at getting what he wanted.

When she took him back, he did not know he had a timeframe to get a divorce. She waited and noticed no changes. His words weren't matching his actions. Eventually this fool says, "Baby, I want YOU! But it's cheaper to keep her and we have kids. Why don't we continue to do us and not worry about her?"

Question: What have you learned from Side Chick 3? How are you going to win him back if you are the main woman? Do you think he honestly loves either of them (the side chick or main chick)? Why?

_____

_____

_____

_____

_____

_____

_____

_____

_____

_____

_____

_____

_____

_____

_____

_____

_____

CHAPTER 2

Benefit of Being a Side Chick Part 1

You must pay to play! Let's be real! Most men are always talking about they refuse to pay to play. They pay the side chick to either keep her quiet, keep her happy and for sex, but it's more than just for money. Below is a list of benefits she has for being the SIDE CHICK:

- Freedom

- Less loneliness

- Time to find a new love

- Minimal drama

- Sex with strings (depends on type of side chick)

- No worries about his whereabouts (depends on type of side chick)

- You might get promoted to main woman

- Ego boost - He risks it all for you

- Get mostly what you want

- You never chase him, he comes for you

Freedom

YES, she is free. She can do whatever she desires in life. The Side Chick does not need anyone's permission to be free…not even his!

You may consult him, if you like or advise him after the fact. At the end of the day, the last word is what you want to do in life.

Main Chick, do you remember what FREEDOM feels like? Think of the time when you were single. You remember now? You never had to consider the consequences or impact of your decisions you made based off of someone else. With him, he's a control fanatic! Men always want to be large and in charge. They want to control your freedom to a certain degree. Don't get me wrong, it's okay to make a man feel needed, but controlling you is another factor.

Look at you now! You're stressed out about him. You have completely lost yourself. Well, you can change that very easily. The Side Chick is living the high life with him. She may boost his ego into making him think he's running things, but in real life, he's NOT running shit. She's running through his money, having good sex and having fun the entire time! When she wakes up in the morning, she has a peace of mind, something you should have.

My goal is for you to have freedom, will power and peace of mind. Focus on you! Once you start living your life for you, watch how things will change within your relationship (if you decide to stay).

Those changes can be for the good and the bad, depending on your relationship. When your relationship changes for the good, you are less stressed. He's getting his act together finally and realizes that YOU are all he needs. He finally will notice the changes in you now. You will STOP NEGLECTING yourself. Your style will change. You'll be going out more with your girlfriends, attending fitness classes, traveling, working on that business you always wanted to start and much more.

On the flip side, he can be rebellious towards your new-found womanhood of freedom. He could hate it! If a man dislikes you having peace of mind, will power and freedom, then leave his ass alone! He is all for himself and will start hating your improvements.

MOVE AROUND ON HIS ASS ASAP!

I'm speaking from my previous experiences! The man I was dealing with got with the program eventually. He had to accept it or get lost. At the time, I was initially a clueless Side Chick that grew into a Combo Side Chick.

I want you to have the Side Chick mind frame of adding freedom to your life. That does not mean do the 'ho-down' life style. Your freedom can be anything that brings positive outcomes in your life. You have become used to living for him, so the transition may not be easy. It will be well worth it at the end. You can add freedom to your life every day- if you want to! It's called "ME TIME." You can pick a couple days out of the week to be completely free and do what you desire. If you have children, leave them with him.

I want you to create a list of 10 things that will add freedom to your life. Every day try at least one of your freedoms. Once you have completed the 10 freedom goals, repeat the list weekly. Your freedom will become a habit over the next 21 to 30 days. It's a good feeling to have freedom over your life.

My Personal Freedom List:

1.

2.

3.

4.

5.

6.

7.

8.

9.

10.

Start TODAY and NOT tomorrow!

Repeat the list when completed until it becomes a habit!

LESS LONELINESS:

The Side Chick is less lonely than the main chick. Her priority is strictly herself. She has open options to ATTEND TO ON A DAILY BASIS. Your friends and family can keep you company sometimes when you are lonely. When I was a Side Chick, I never was too lonely. From time to time I would call a few of my male friends for conversations or a friendly date. The relationship with them was strictly platonic. Even then, platonic male contact was limited. I would hang out with friends and family most of time. I actually had a LIFE! My aunt would host dinners or BBQs all the time. It was a good feeling to be around people who honestly LOVE you! I would have a girls night gathering for the entire week-end at my house, which was super lit. We would have food, drinks, games and great conversations about our lives. The point I'm trying to make is that the Side Chick was never sitting around crying and acting lifeless because of "her man."

Stop sitting around feeling sorry for yourself! Stop feeling hopeless and lonely. If he's not giving you the attention, connecting with you emotionally, he's draining your positivity. "***Pizzazz*** his ass."

Go out and enjoy life with those who love you.

If you decide to stay or walk away, sometimes you may get lonely on those late nights and desire some comfort. When you're in that place then pray to God to remove that needy spirit. Ask God and keep asking him to remove that lonely spirit. Read Psalms 25:16 which states, "Turn to me and be gracious to me, for I am lonely and afflicted." After praying to God, then make a plan to not be lonely all the time. Sometimes you have to pick up that phone and just start making plans.

Repeat after me:

"God please remove this lonely phase out of my life. Help me move forward. Help me do what makes me happy and fulfilled. Keep me closer to my loved ones and allow me to be free."

Keep pushing forward. The Side Chick is not feeling lonely and depressed like you.

Create a list of 5 things you can do to replace that lonely feeling:

1.

2.

3.

4.

5.

Time on Her Hands to Find New Love

I'm not suggesting you cheat if you're married and deciding to stay with him. I am strongly recommending you prepare your mind and open your heart to a fresh breath of new love.

You have to evaluate your relationship. Is it worth fighting for? Is it too far gone? You must consider and prepare to get back out there. The Side Chick has freedom to move around in the love department. She's not dealing with the BS that you are entertaining on a daily basis. She's attending networking events, happy hours, vacations with guys and much more. It's time for you to do the same.

I am the type to fight for my relationship. I'll go to the killing floor for mine- IF it's worth it. Sometimes we have to just let it go. Do not fight for your relationship if he has repeat patterns of deal breakers that you just can't handle. You have to decide if you want a new man in your life or not. Our goal is to embrace and be embraced by actual love in our relationship.

Once I gave up being the Side Chick, I made a list of things I wanted in a man. I started a plan on how to get that type of man too. My new search process has been going well so far. Maybe my next book will be about my new-found love! Now, it's your turn.

Below write 10 things you want in a man. Please be realistic! Compare those points to your current man's characteristics and traits. Discuss them with your man. Where he's lacking, find out if he's willing to meet you half way to change something about himself before you WALK AWAY. If not, start a NOW HIRING process for the man that will. What men say, "What you won't do another woman will." That same rule applies to him as well.

1.

2.

3.

4.

5.

6.

7.

8.

9.

10.

So, what happened? What was his response when you asked about meeting you half way?

_____

_____

_____

_____

_____

_____

_____

No Drama:

The Side Chick comes with no drama. I'm not saying you are a drama queen, and extra type of chick at all. It's just that he's so busy trying to cover up his double life that he keeps her happy and she is perceived as drama-free to him. Most guys consider the Side Chick the "fun girl," a.k.a. drama-free. I want to you stand up to him when it's needed but back down on the unnecessary bitching. Think of the times when you started arguments with him just because you were having a bad day or you just wanted to piss him off. Well, he's comparing moments like that against his Side Chick. You're just pushing him more towards her!

Write four things that can lead you into a drama free relationship with him. On date night, discuss it with him. I bet you two will be able to eliminate some drama. However, you must be open and LISTEN to him! Do NOT over speak him! Allow him to express himself as long as he respects you in the process!

1.

2.

3.

4.

Not Worrying About Break-Ups

This benefit is honestly good for Side Chick#2. Side Chick #1 and Side Chick #3 may be worried about breaking up because the relationship is somewhat real and emotions are deep on both ends. Side Chick #2 does not care if he stops talking to her or not. She gets what she can get and moves around on his ass. They both have a clear understanding because she is aware of you. If they stop messing around she "may" be hurt or sad for a quick second, but she has other options available to her.

On the flip side, you, as the Main Chick, are worrying about breaking up. When you're worrying about the relationship ending, it can add more stress to your life. If your relationship is coming to an end then cry it out and BOSS up on his ass. It is human nature to become sad or depressed after a bad breakup. However, we are not supposed to be bitter for the rest of our lives!

SEX WITH NO STRINGS ATTACHED:

The only Side Chick that can actually benefit from this 100% with no real emotions is Side Chick #2. She is having a wild sex life with your man. There's just no telling what she's doing in the bedroom. Men are very visually minded individuals. This Side Chick is down for whatever in the bedroom and may teach him something too. She takes care of your man visually and sexually. Most of my male friends say sex is boring after a while because it's like a line dance. They said it's straight up repetition with the main chick and they get bored after a while.

Some women may not feel comfortable or are not satisfied with their bodies. Girl, a man does not care if you are fat with stretch marks. They just want to release that build up at the end of the day. When I was the Side Chick #3, I was a little nasty thing and that's all I'm going to say. I started to learn his body completely and began to satisfy him all over. As soon as he walked in the house, I would go straight in. He wasn't prepared or ready for that action at all. The point that I'm trying to make is keep your sex life spicy. To be honest, I believe that our sex life was 50% of why he kept missing me.

I had his mind so wrapped up in my sex game. That man did something to me because I became a pro! Guess what? That was his weak spot. Once again, act like the Side Chick in the bedroom. Go crazy girl! Mess his head up completely. Good sex can take you very far in your relationship.

CHAPTER 3

Benefits of A Side Chick Part 2

NOT WORRYING ABOUT WHERE HE IS

By nature, women tend to worry about where her dick or man is located by the clock. However, it's not cool knowing where he is at all times. Be like Side Chick #2 and not care about where he is all the time. As long as he is available for when you need him, then that's all that matters. Are you the type that your man must check in with you on every move he makes? Stop doing that to him! Sometimes he may need a little space and privacy. When men feel like we're questioning them like the FBI, it will push them away. It's okay to call and check on him sometimes, but stop sweating him 24/7. Allow him to miss you sometimes.

Let me give you a little story behind what happened with me. It was January 5th of 2017 and my ex (the cheater) wanted to meet up with me. Around this time, I had left him six months prior due to me finding out about his "marriage." I graduated from the Clueless Side Chick #1 to Side Chick #2. Mentally, I thought I had moved on from our relationship. I was in a happy space at that time. I was very curious about what he wanted to talk about. As I was driving to meet him at the shopping mall, I started getting very nervous. All my emotions started to come back instantly. When I saw him, he was ill with a cold and very emotional about us breaking up. He had a temperature of 102! Suddenly, all of the sympathy toward him came rushing over me. Word of advice ladies, **a man will crawl out his sick bed just to con you**. Don't fall for it like I did. Let's just say we had "the talk." While we were talking, his wife kept blowing up his phone. After the 4th phone call, he picks up and expressed his irritation with her. She was so loud over the phone. I heard everything she said to him. She was mad because he didn't tell her where he was going. He was actually going to buy some stuff for his daughter from the mall for school. After he hung up the phone, he expressed that she always does that to him and it's pushing him more away from her. And eventually she pushed him so much that he came back into my life.

Ladies, if you want to know where he is all the time, then you will have an issue on your hand. Men hate being questioned like they are in an FBI interrogation. If you want freedom than give him some freedom too. If you have to continue to call him and know his whereabouts all the damn time, then leave his ass alone. You don't trust him! Why be with someone who you can't trust at all? There's no point in being the FBI all time.

YOU MIGHT BE THE MAIN WOMAN NEXT

This benefit is a hard pill to take ladies. Between Side Chick #1 and Side Chick #3, you may lose him completely. He has fallen in love with her and is willing to risk it all for her now. He is head over heels for her now. So, yes being a Side Chick can lead into being the Main Woman. Some people say how you get him is how you lose him. Well, that story is not always true. People are placed in your life for a reason and for a season. I could have taken him from her if I really wanted to but I'm no home wrecker. I gave him a time frame and he didn't move fast enough so I moved on to something better and new.

EGO BOOSTER

This benefit applies for Side Chick #2 and Side Chick #3. He makes her feel like she is worth the risk of him losing everything. She is his Nobel Prize. When I first found out that he was married, I was pissed. In parts of my mind I did feel honored that he would risk so much for me. My ego was on cloud 10. I knew that was a bad feeling so I disregarded that feeling instantly. However, the man does boost his Side Chick's ego.

Let your ego soar. When you leave the hair salon you feel absolutely beautiful. Embrace that feeling and incorporate it into your ego. Get like Jill Scott says, "Live Your Life Like it's Golden." Be your own ego booster.

SHE HAS THE UPPER HAND AND GETS WHAT SHE WANTS

This area is a winning area for all Side Chicks! He wants to keep her happy because she keeps him happy, even if it's just sex! If she needed her bills paid or wants a date night, then he's coming! She is his personal "fix it" in all areas. He gives her what she wants because he's living a double life and wants to keep it that way.

When I was dealing with him, I had whatever I wanted. I can honestly say I barely heard the word no. He kept my bills paid and gave me money for whatever along with happiness. (Until the drama jumped off). It wasn't always about the money either with him. Sometimes we just wanted to relax in the house and watch TV all day. Sometimes I just wanted to hear his voice and see his face. He was there for me when I needed him! Even when our schedules conflicted, he would find a way.

The reason I got whatever I wanted from him was because I

became an important asset to him.

Ladies, become an asset to him in all areas. I did whatever for him when he needed me to a certain point. Sometimes I felt like his personal assistant because I was INVESTED with him. I knew all of his personal information, his deep secrets, his pains and much more. We shared so much together that he couldn't say no to me. We shared too much for him to say no. I'm not proud of that relationship, but I did have the upper hand. I was an asset to him mentally, physically, and financially.

SHE NEVER CHASED HIM BECAUSE HE COMES FOR HER

This benefit applies to all Side Chicks. He continues to chase her regardless if she knows or not. She can walk away anytime she wants in the relationship. The ball is in her hand honestly because if she is truly done with him, then she would not allow him to come back. Women love the chase from a man. She makes him feel non-important sometimes to keep him on his toes.

Situation:

When I was dealing with him, he stayed chasing me. When we broke up, I was done with him completely. I walked away on faith. I kept thinking about all the lies about him being married. Every blue moon we would talk for like 2 minutes tops and ran into each other at public events. On January 1, 2017, I was at John Hannah's 11:30am service. I wanted a better New Year for 2017. At this point I was well over him. Don't get me wrong, I did miss him and still felt like I loved him deeply.

I prayed to God for what to do with him and help me to keep moving forward. My motto was "Out of sight and out of mind."

My mind was becoming that after a while. During prayer, why did he call me multiple times? I thought I saw a ghost or something in church. I ended up texting him after church. Deep down inside I was happy because they always come back. I still stand where I stand. Later that night he was going to come over to my family's house to eat gumbo. Of course, he had some sort of excuse. A few days later we met up at the shopping mall and had that "talk."

I didn't go chasing him! He came for me. I was good where I was. Of course, he had this plan in place for us and wanted to move forward 100% with me. I took him back and it was amazing while it lasted.

All Side Chicks are not bad in my eyes, depending on the situation because he comes for her at the end of the day. Why be mad at her and not him? The man actually does chase them and begs for them to come back. They create a plan and put all cards on the table.

I am not an advocate for or against being a side chick. I am an advocate for the benefits I outlined in this book. Ladies, I hope this section was an eye opener for you. I've listed the benefits below again for your convenience. Take a few notes on what you've learned in this section:

✓ Freedom

✓ Less loneliness

✓ Time to find a new love

✓ Minimal drama

✓ Sex with strings (depends on type of side chick)

✓ No worries about his whereabouts (depends on type of side chick)

- ✓ You might get promoted to main woman
- ✓ Ego boost - He risks it all for you
- ✓ Get mostly what you want
- ✓ You never chase him, he comes for you

CHAPTER 4

The Types of Men Who are Attracted to Side Chicks

Not all men are attracted to Side Chicks. I have some male friends who have never cheated or stepped out on their woman. This section is tricky because it depends on what's going on with the Main Woman. If he's not happy and tired of trying to communicate with you, then he may step out.

I do have my own personal theory about the type of man that may step out on his wife or woman but everyone has their own opinion in this area.

Type A: He wants another woman to please him where his woman lacks. The lacks can be sexually or attention to his life goals and aspirations **(remember- become an asset).**

Type B: He has a good foundation at home but is greedy. He wants his cake and ice cream at all times.

My ex was a combination of both to a certain degree. He had a loving family, a house: both had careers, two children, and much more. From our conversations we had, she was lacking in so many areas. I was an asset and threw down in the love making department. Before I knew he had all of that going, I never felt it was another woman for years. He hid his situation very well.

Life is too short to settle and keep hurting each other mentally. My ex claimed he was so mad and upset with his wife, but he never left her. I do believe he loves her dearly because they have been married for 10 years. The more time you're in a toxic situation, the more time you're wasting in life.

Type A Man:

This man can be very dangerous! He has a strong appetite for something that is missing from home. In most cases, it may be sex. However, he may be lacking companionship, feelings, time, attention, man power, and much more.

If Side Chick #1 and Side Chick #3 continue to feed him what he's missing, then it would be harder for him to walk away from any one of those chicks.

When a woman learns what a man is craving and knows his weak spots, then it's a wrap. I was giving my ex great sex and attention, and I catered to him to a certain point. I was his rider until the end. Sometimes he would have me do stuff that I felt that his wife was supposed to help him with. For example, I am very big on credit and my financial well-being. He was the type who paid cash for everything and knew little about credit. I helped him balance his financial well-being and improved his credit from bad to good. That wasn't my job, but I did it because I cared and I knew it was going to benefit us long term (before I knew about the wife).

I was able to help him learn how to grow his money and think big.

According to him, financial strength and growth were not a part of their relationship.

Ladies, learn your man's appetites. Pay close to attention to him and start studying him. Sometimes test certain things out with him and see his reaction. Below I want you to write a list of things you think are his appetites. Next, do a research project on him to see if all your answers are correct. Once you have fully completed this exercise, then apply it to your relationship. See if things will turn around.

1.

2.

3.

4.

5.

6.

7.

8.

9.

10.

Type B Man:

Having this type of man in your life is very dangerous for various reasons. He is super greedy and does not care about anyone but himself. He has a happy foundation at home, but wants more. One woman can never satisfy him. Shit, you better be careful and make sure he's not into the same sex either. Type B is very sneaky and knows how to control your mind.

In public, he is an awesome man to his family and vice-versa. Behind closed doors, he wants more and can't have enough ladies. His Main Woman is giving him all the business from the bedroom to catering to his needs. He will never be happy with himself. Men like this need attention from everyone and want to "feel" important in society. A friend of mine dealt with a guy who was exactly like Type B. He had a loving family, good money, and was perfect in her eyes. What's done in the dark will come to light one day. He was a very bad guy behind closed doors. He had a baby on her and an entire new life. He told her that one woman could not make him happy. She was very hurt but she found the strength to walk away.

Both types of these men are not the kind of man you need in your life. I want you to recognize certain traits with both men like them. I'm not telling you to leave your man, but your happiness comes first.

Types A & B are dangerous men to even be with anyway. Type A has major lack of communication skills and Type B is a plain right out Greedy HOE! Ladies, no man is perfect but know your worth. If you can connect to this chapter then ask God to remove them out of your life before you "commit" a crime.

Answer these questions for me and yourself:

Are you holding on to Type A or Type B in your relationship?

How are you handling the bad issues with him?

Why do you stay?

Does he make you feel special after he gets caught?

Did you know he was lying but the lie was so good, you gave him a pass?

How many times have you gone through this with him?

If you walked away, how did you do it?

What did you learn?

Would you be able to recognize Type A and Type B in the near future?

What qualities are you NOT trying to have with your next relationship?

What qualities do you want in your next relationship?

Are you stronger now mentally?

Can you walk away?

Ladies, I want you to recognize the Fuck Boy that comes into your life. For those of you who don't know, my definition of a Fuck Boy is a "boy" who has no morals or values in life. He basically fits in where he gets in. When it comes to women, he does not respect them at all. Stay away from him because he will mess your life up.

Back in the Day Stories About Fuck Boys and Me

When I was younger I dealt with so many guys cheating and lying to me. I started experiencing BS from men starting at the age of 16 years old. I attended Morgan high school in Chicago, IL. My very first drama relationship was with a guy named Jay. He was on the track team. He was older than me. Back in the day, dating an upper classman was the new trend for the younger girls in High School. I never knew about his hoeish ways because I was in the IB Program. All IB students stayed together for all classes from freshman year to sophomore year. We never had integrated classes with the other students. I was only able to see Jay in between classes, maybe lunch, after school, and some weekends.

I was so crazy about this boy. We would have long talks at night on the phone almost every night. I remember on Valentine's Day he gave me a rose and a card that took my soul away. At the end of the card, he said he loved me. That is where Jay messed up with me. I never knew anything about love with a guy until I met him. Around the spring time is when all hell broke out with him. At that time, we were dating for almost 9 months. I was not sexually active at all with him or with anyone. I was a pure virgin at the age of 16.

I heard that he was kissing another girl who was on the track team. Well, she didn't have the best reputation at all. Let's just say she was very "active" in high school. When I heard about her and him, I immediately addressed him, and he denied it instantly. I knew he was lying so I approached her. She knew we were together because our relationship was no secret. As soon as I was passing periods outside, I ran up to her and tried to beat her up. My plan failed because she ran away. He broke my heart so bad. I remember talking to him and he made it seem like I was tripping. I eventually stopped talking to him maybe a week later. He was my very first "Fuck Boy."

Did I lose myself ladies? Hell No!! I was young and didn't really care. I was hurt for maybe three days and moved on super easily. What if we can have that same mind frame with our men today? I could have been a dummy, stayed with him and took his BS. I'm glad I left him alone because lord knows what could have happened if I stayed. When was your first "Fuck Boy?"

Shortly after our breakup I met another guy name Dee. He went to Curry High School; he was a pretty boy. He was 5'6, perfectly arched eyebrows, smooth light- brown skin, deep black wavy hair, well dressed, and very romantic. All girls at most Chicago High Schools wanted him because he was very popular. My family loved him too.

He used to come over and watch movies with me all the time. We even went on cute romantic dates. Our first date was on the CTA bus to Ford City to the movies. After our first date, I knew he was the one. At that point, I completely forgot about Jay. I was 17 years old by this time when I started dating Dee. Literally after 6 months of dating Dee I lost my virginity. In between those 6 months I did encounter one situation with a girl named Cookie. It was nothing major from my understanding so I gave him a pass.

Dee worked at McDonalds as a part time cashier in Chicago. I really did not care too much about his job because all the girls liked him. I remember when I first heard about Cookie. I skipped my

After-School Program to pop up at his house. I did a lot of lying to my auntie to get to his house.

When I arrived at his house, his mom lied and said he was not at home. I found out she was lying and I busted through the house and saw both of them in the kitchen. I instantly went crazy. She was considered Side Chick #2 because she knew of me.

This is where it gets super juicy!

One day I received a call from a guy saying he was Dee's lover. I thought it was a joke because Dee was not gay at all. However, this guy knew too many details about me. The boy worked at McDonalds with him as a cook.

I went to his job on Dee's off day to confront the young man. At this time, we had basic small block cell phones. He showed me all the text messages to prove his accusations. How did I feel!? I was so hurt that I damn near wanted to die. I lost my virginity to an undercover "fuck boy."

How did I recover from this pain at such as early age? I told my aunt, prayed to God to forgive me, and focused on me. I started back focusing on me completely. I started going back to dance classes, hanging out with friends, and staying around positive people. This situation helped me become wiser at an early age about certain qualities in Fuck Boys.

At the age of 18, you couldn't tell me anything because I was making over $2,500 a month and a full-time college student at Purdue University. My next actual "adult" relationship didn't happen until I was 18 years old. Let's just say we didn't last long either. When I saw BS from him, I ran away and left on the next train smoking.

In the midst of that two- second relationship, I met a guy named Rico. I met Rico at a club named Bi-Level. I remember when Lil' Wayne had a song called "Make it Rain." Back then, throwing money in the club was cool. I remember dancing on him and he started throwing hundreds at me. I collected like $500 and his number. From that point, I was head over heels for Rico.

I moved in with him shortly after dating him for three months. He gave me the world until drugs entered our relationship. He started popping pills and started putting his hands on me. I was in a very bad situation. I lost my job and dropped out of college because of him. I lost myself damn near completely. I felt like I needed him.

Ladies, have you encountered a relationship that you were stuck in and lost everything?

I went through so much drama with him that I had to walk away. This topped off all my pain I went through from previous relationships. I lost friends, family, myself and almost my future. I used to wonder why would he cheat on me or put his hands on me. Why couldn't he stay loyal? I was doing everything right by him. Now that I'm 30 years old, I realize that we were too young for love, but he had no right to beat on me.

He was considered Type B. One woman could not make him happy. I had to put my game face on and turn a negative situation into a positive situation. I learned so much from this relationship that it has truly molded me into the woman I am today. After our break-up, I did encounter a few bumps with other men but I was able to walk away cold turkey.

I had to remember why God placed me here on earth. I was not placed here on earth to be unhappy and sad all the time over a man. Men and women need each other. However, rules do apply to both sides to order to be successful. I did try to work out all my bad relationships to the point I lowered my standards for a man when I was younger.

It's okay to change your viewpoints on certain relationship issues but only to a certain degree. If you're enduring pain, then it's not worth it. We all have made those mistakes where we would give in and do whatever to make him happy. Stop it now!! Step your game up and don't take another heart break.

Examine every relationship that went bad. Learn to turn the negative into a positive learning experience. It's a discovery learning process at the end of the day. You may have not met Mr. Perfect but you can recognize Fuck Boy shit from a mile away. I want you to stay true to yourself and love living your life.

Values You Carry About Yourself:

Below, make a list of values you carry about yourself that you are not willing to change. Stick to your values and post them around your house or workplace to remind yourself every day. I use sticky notes in my bedroom to remind myself of who I am at all times.

1.

2.

3.

4.

5.

6.

7.

8.

9.

10.

Sometimes your past Fuck Boy may try to pop back up. Just remind yourself of what happened and remember he does not respect your values. Stay strong and move forward in life.

CHAPTER 5

Why Me?

Guess what? Nobody can give you an actual answer except you! Why did it happen to you? Did you slack up in your relationship? Did you forget to value yourself? Were you open-minded? Were you selfish? Did you have bad intentions or motives in the relationship?

Sometimes women tend to blame themselves for why the man cheated. Sometimes it may not be you. If you know that you have truly done everything in your relationship, then it's not you. Sometimes a relationship can get boring. Especially if the both of you are living life like robots. Sometimes it's okay to be open to change.

In one of my past relationships I was cheated on and it was my fault. I was there physically but mentally I was completely gone. I was working 40 hours or more a week, doing a part time internship, clubbing and had a side hustle. I was an on and off girlfriend. Sometimes I would talk to him all day and spend lots of time with him. Most of the time I was putting him last. Our relationship was just too serious for me at the time. All I wanted was fun. I was stressed out from my personal life. I wanted him to be my dream gateway vacation all the time. He was not able to light that torch in my world. He was a good man, but was too serious.

I was 24 years old and was living life to the fullest. I loved him dearly but I was not ready to be "the one" for him. I was obsessively into myself. I didn't give that relationship the time one gives a serious one. Eventually, he started cheating on me with other women. At one point, I didn't care because I was somewhat done with our relationship. After a while, I started to change my lifestyle. I stopped clubbing as much. I added structure to my life. By then it was too late. He was into someone else. I tried my best to win him back but it was too late.

Another woman gave him the attention I didn't. I kept asking myself, "Why Me?" I knew the answer to that question. After truthful inner reflection, I acknowledged that I was the problem. I was an absent girlfriend. I left him wide open to ANY TYPE of side chick. I allowed a good man to get away. However, I'm a firm believer that God places people in your life for a season and a reason. He was one of many lessons. I made a promise to myself that when I'm in a relationship worth keeping, I'm going to bring it-100 percent.

As women, we seem to know all the answers, except the answer as to why he cheated. Reflection on yourself is very important in this chapter. I want you to reflect on who you are as a woman. Nobody is perfect; however, you know your relationship's flaws.

After my last breakup, I was able to reflect on who is Shanti Helena is. I noticed that I did not value myself as I should have. When you do not know your value, others will see that. God, why me? What did I do? I did everything in my power!

After I took some months to reflect on myself, I noticed that I didn't value myself or even believe in myself as a woman. Men can see right through us. They will see the weakness. I believe he saw that I did not know my value and did not value myself enough. I would allow people to walk all over me and disrespect me. I wanted to feel needed. I did not want any issues or have to address any issues with anyone. I used to be a firecracker but I had calmed down way too much. He knew he could get away with making me his Side Chick.

Situation:

Rachel met her man in elementary school. They were together on and off for 20 years. They did not have any children. While they were studying in college together, he stressed her out so badly. He was a cheater. She was studying to be a doctor. She never left his side no matter what. However, their relationship has a deep secret nobody knew about. They both slept with other people as long each other knew about it. They had an open relationship. She honestly did not want an open relationship, but she wanted to keep him happy. He would bring other women home while she was in a different room watching TV. They did this for years. As they began to get older, it started to become a problem.

Eventually he started sleeping with other women without her knowing. One night she was studying and he brought home some young girl from the club. She was so heated and mad to the point she went off on the girl as well. Rachel had enough. As a matter of fact she had way too much. She left him.

When she moved out, she found a new her and a new life. She questioned herself, "Why Me?" She knew the answer to that question to begin with. She allowed him to get away with so much and never had boundaries in their relationship.

How would you have handled this situation from the very beginning?

When men cheat, they have a choice to make. Cheating shows a lack of character because they are willing to break the trust between you two. If he cheated on you, he does not value your committed relationship. He may value a committed relationship based on many factors of his life. He has lacked love from his mother, family, or from his upbringing in general. Or, he simply is a hoe?

Are you emotionally satisfied with him? If not, then that's another reason why he may cheat on you. Men have emotions, too. They need that connection with you. Sometimes men will not tell a woman when something is wrong. We have to read in between the lines to understand what is going on. If you act like you do not care then that could possibly affect him.

Another reason why he may cheat with a Side Chick is because emotionally the relationship is over and neither one wants to admit it. Move on and find someone new, otherwise you will keep asking yourself, *Why Me?*

I want you to avoid asking yourself "Why Me?" If you have asked yourself "Why Me?" too many times and he's still cheating, then remove yourself right away. God has a way of showing us things in our life. Sometimes God will show us something that would hurt so badly but it will help us in the long run. No relationship is perfect and some may be worth saving.

Wouldn't it be nice to finally meet someone who was all yours? He is all your man. Having that good feeling knowing that your man would not step out on you is one of the best feelings in the world. When you're happy in a relationship, it will reflect in your everyday life. You would smile more and be happier about your life. Never settle for less!

Season People

Sometimes just because you're with a man for years does not mean he's the one. Some people are brought into our lives for a season. Was he brought into your life to teach you some things about yourself or just a life lesson? That person can bring joy, happiness, sadness, and/or pain. I can rant on about how many of the men I was with who cheated on me. However, each man taught me a valuable lesson about myself.

Why do you think this man was placed in your life? After being the Side Chick for years, I learned a lot. He was brought into my life so I can see me and change myself. He could have been brought in my life for other reasons as well. He made me open my eyes about good things and bad things. I'll share one good and one bad with you. On a good note, that man encouraged me to be about my hustle. I stepped up my entrepreneurial game. On another note, I learned to pay attention to my instinct. I learned to listen to the little voices inside that nagged me. It was telling me something's not quite right; there's a missing part to his life. I now know not to hide my head in the sand like an ostrich. You have to face and confront those things that make you wonder and feel uneasy. There could be a whole family hiding in the shadow of his lie.

CHAPTER 6

Open Communications

Touch, taste, sound, sight and COMMUNICATION! That is the sixth sense- or at least should be. It certainly is the key to life and longevity. Ladies, since communication is essential to survival, it most certainly is a very necessary thing between you and your man.

If something is going down that makes you feel bad, sad or you just don't like, don't bottle it up. You must talk about it. Make your feelings known. He may bring you roses when you'd rather have lilies. Tell the man. He doesn't have ESP. If you want him to move that thing a little to left to hit that G spot, you got to let him know.

If your man is acting shady and starting to change in ways that are not good for your relationship, talk to him about those things. You must find out what's going on with him. The best way to do that is to get it from him. His reason and rationale is in him. It may not be easy or comfortable to have some discussions, but it is necessary for the survival of your relationship.

In relationships there must be compromise. In order to get there you must know what and why. In order to get there you must communicate. There is power in information. Get inside his mind as well as his heart.

CHAPTER 7

Boss Up Your Life

Now what? You either decided to stay or you left. However, you lost yourself as well. After my last relationship ended, I completely lost it mentally, physically, and spiritually. I stopped going to church, gained weight and my hair was a hot mess. I didn't care about my appearance, stopped hustling for my goals, barely hung out with friends and almost gave up on life completely. At the time of our final breakup, I had just lost my job. My friendships were rocky, I was having family issues, and my home caught on fire before Thanksgiving. There was a lot going on in 2017 for me; I was so drained.

He had promised that he would help me. He didn't. It was the lowest point of my life. How could he do this to me at a time like this? I never left his side when he was down! After I prayed about it and cried about it, I had to Boss up my life completely and focus on me. Your situation may be different from mine. You may have decided to stay and work it out; however, you lost yourself during the process. Girl, it's time to get what you deserve the most, which is creating your new life.

2 Corinthians 12:9-10

9 But he said to me, "My grace is sufficient for you, for my power is made perfect in weakness." Therefore I will boast all the more gladly about my weaknesses, so that Christ's power may rest on me.

10 That is why, for Christ's sake, I delight in weaknesses, in insults, in hardships, in persecutions, in difficulties. For when I am weak, then I am strong.

Psalm 28:7-8 NIV

7 The LORD is my strength and my shield; my heart trusts in him, and he helps me. My heart leaps for joy, and with my song I praise him.

8 The LORD is the strength of his people, a fortress of salvation for his anointed one.

I grew up in Church my entire life. I used to attend church at least two to three times a week. I was part of the youth programs and sang too. I knew that no matter how horrible things got in my life, I would always praise God, through the good and the bad.

During my battles, I forgot about God to a certain extent. I used to wonder about the man I was dating. I was so busy chasing him that I neglected my relationship with God. Guess what? God never gave up on me. Every night before I went to bed, I used to ask God to show me signs about this man. I prayed for him to show me even if it would hurt my feelings. I needed to know. When you pray, mean it. Get ready, God will answer prayer. After months of praying and asking him for answers, all that man's bad sides started hitting me from left to right, all in my face. I couldn't handle it! I just woke up one Sunday morning and went to John Hannah's 11:30am service and gave God praise. That particular Sunday service was literally about me. He was preaching about sleeping with someone else's man and allowing a man to use you to his advantage. I knew at that given moment, it was over for us. I cried so heavy in church that Sunday morning, asking God to heal me and help me get out.

I knew I had to make some changes in my life. I had started picking up bad habits such as drinking and smoking heavily. I even started hanging out with the wrong crowd of people for a while. After attending a few Sunday services and Bible Studies, I started creating fasting sessions every week. Each week I would sacrifice something for God.

What are you willing to give up for God? Below list 10 things you want to give up. You can do it weekly or monthly!

1.

2.

3.

4.

5.

6.

7.

8.

9.

10.

Once I started fasting on a regular basis and kept going to church, I started watching my life change slowly for the good. Sometimes everything that God does for us may seem bad, but the outcome is greater. For a long time, I did not understand why I lost my job. I was put in a very uncomfortable situation where I could not afford to be lazy. I had to pay $4,000 a month in bills alone. I started creating multiple streams of income for myself. Since I lost my job, I'm making more money not working for anyone else!

I give all my praise to God because he pushed me in a very uncomfortable place to make me a better woman. If you are in the same situation as I was, then you can do it as well. A good prayer can take you a long way. Sometimes you may think God is not listening, but he is and always will. He may not move when you want him to-but you must be very patient.

Sometimes I used to wonder if God even heard me crying. I would be so furious, because time was running out and I had no options left. Just when I was ready to give up, he came right through for me.

Testimony:

I was working in corporate for a well-known hotel in Chicago for two years. I outgrew my job and wanted something better. I started working as a Director at the YMCA on the South Side. I thought that was my dream career at the time. Unfortunately, they felt I wasn't a good fit and let me go. I was very disappointed because I had a stable job before this one. I could have stayed at my last job if I had known this would happen.

However, after being terminated, many doors of opportunity started to open up for me. I would have never written this book if I was still working at the YMCA! I started to get checks in the mail all of a sudden. Most of all, I started a new hustle for myself. Never say what you would never do for some money! I started driving for Lyft full time, worked as the Marketing Director for H&B Catering & Events, managed my own small business consulting company, worked part time as a driver for an organic food company, and worked small events for third party companies. I was working 5 different jobs on a daily basis just to survive. I am happy and blessed that I was able to keep a roof over my head and all of my bills paid.

I was focused on ME! Yes, I have two degrees, a Masters and Bachelors, but that didn't stop me from hustling at all. I could have accepted another "job" but I didn't. I was able to create my own schedule and focus on my personal goals. All of those jobs allowed me to create my own schedule. At first, I was humiliated and embarrassed about these jobs. After all, I have two higher education degrees. But, God made a way for me. I have to remember that at the end of the day! He could have left me in the dark and only He knows what could have happened to me next. Never be ashamed of what your job may be! Be glad for the income and do it in a spirit of excellence. God has it all planned out for you hon! Just sit back and watch!

Getting Fit

Every woman's goal is to be healthy and fit. However, life will get in the way of that. You may have children to attend to or just a busy life style. During my last relationship, I gained so much weight due to stress. Most women gain weight during the happy season of their relationship. I am the total opposite! When my relationships are doing great I actually lose weight and start glowing. When my relationship is going bad, then I would gain weight. I cannot just blame my "bad" relationships on why I gained weight either. I must blame myself for allowing a non-factor in my life to get the best of me. I had to let those bad food habits go and start making changes. During my transition, I lost my identity of who Shanti Helena was.

I was tired of looking like crap! All my pants were too small and my love handles were out of control too. I was tired of men saying, "You cute but on the big girl side." I have nothing against big women but my body was out of its comfort zone. When I would causally go out on dates with guys, I felt like shit! The more I kept complaining, I knew I had to make some changes in my life.

My finances were not the best but I had to make sacrifices to afford a gym membership and a personal trainer. I had $500 of free money to do whatever I wanted. At first, I was going to take a mini weekend getaway but I had to reconsider my plan. I paid $250 for my personal trainer for 30 days and the rest was spent on my gym membership.

"If you want change then you are the only one who can change your problem!"

After my first two days, I was ready to give up. During my workout sessions, I kept thinking about how my ex- boyfriends played me to the left and always talked about me being a big girl. When you're working out, think about the good and bad. On the good side, I was thinking about when I bump into my ex-boyfriend in the streets

"Oh, I bet he will be all over me but I'm stronger now baby. Move around fuck boy!"

I know it can be hard to get your body up early in the morning and to eat healthy. Let's face it girl, once your body starts being on point, your confidence will be on fleek! When your husband or man starts saying, "Damn baby look at your fine ass," it will be worth it. In the back of your head I bet you're thinking, "Yeah, if you think this shit, then imagine what other dudes are thinking too."

In order to be successful in this department of fitness you need discipline and time management. You need to create a schedule that is best for you and stick to it no matter what. If you are invited to a friend's birthday dinner, order healthy food off the menu. In addition, I stopped drinking completely for 60 days.

My Personal Plan:

- ✓ Workout: 3 Days a week (Drink 8 bottles of water daily)

- ✓ Food Diet Plan: Veggies, Detox Smoothies, & Meal Prep Weekly

- ✓ Sleep: Get at least 6 to 8 hours of sleep daily

- ✓ Morning Motivation: Listen to a Motivational Speaker for 5 minutes every morning and before you go to bed

Before: After:

New Hair Style:

If you know me personally, then you know I originally had long hair. I woke up one morning and just wanted a new look. I was unsure what I wanted at first. I wanted something that spoke I'm BOLD, INDEPENDENT, FIRM, SEXY, and BAD AS HELL. My hair stylist Diamond recommended that I cut all my hair off and start over completely. When my hair was cut off completely, I compared that to a new life and beginnings. It was a fresh feeling to have. Now that your body is on point and you have a new hair style to rock, GIRL you are WINNING!

Before you just change your hair style, make sure to have a proper consultation with your hair stylist. I want you to look great! If you decided to stay with him then change the game up on him. YOU are a new woman and ready to take charge at the world.

Before: After:

New Wardrobe:

There's nothing like a brand-new look! During my transition of bossing up, I wanted to find this new look that was different from my normal look. I had to stride out of my comfort zone. At the time money was an issue, but I kept coupons on me. My favorite store was Express. Express has so many different looks and good quality. I started buying skinny jeans with oversized dress shirts and blazers. Oversize dress shirts were perfect for me because I was still trying to lose weight at the time. I would wear a skinny belt on top of the shirt. Ladies, you can never go wrong with a blazer as well. I wanted that casual sexy business look. To top off the outfits, I had popping colors-and pointy- toe heels.

When you go shopping for something new to wear, you will feel great. At first, I would say, "Well, it's not like I have a man anymore or somewhere to go looking this good." I was still feeling a little bitter about my breakup but shortly after, I said, "F this, I'm about to step out every chance I get." Ladies, we have a major problem of buying so many new clothes and never going anywhere. If you are single and want some sort of male attention, then how would he know about you when you stay in the house all the time?

After you get your hair, nails, and make up with your new outfit-GIRL, you will feel like you're on cloud 10! Now, it's time to actually go and mingle and show yourself off to the world. I just want to create this NEW you starting today! If you can't afford anything expensive, then shop somewhere more affordable. Sometimes I would shop at the second-hand stores and I would luck up on some good stuff. When you walk in that house and he sees how freaking sexy you are and you have a new look, BOOM! GIR-L YOU AT THE TOP! There's nothing like having your power back from a man. Remember that. However, the key is to keep that power and never let his ass have it again!

So, what are we doing today ladies?

Going Shopping For A New Look!

Creating a Business Plan:

If you know me personally then you know I'm all about starting a business. So far, I have one business under my belt. I own the *Shanti Helena* brand. In the past, I owned over 5 businesses and none of them went very far. None of my previous businesses ever went far because I was all over the place and wasn't sure what I wanted. I had to find something where I can connect with my followers and sell an amazing product. The best product to sell is something that everyone can relate to. Eventually, that's how I came up with "Why Side Chicks Winning?" book and the *Shanti Helena* brand.

I want to help you elevate your finances this year and expand your net worth. Below are 5 steps to help you get your idea started:

1. Train your mind to identify areas of opportunities.

2. Start making lists of problems that need solving.

3. Come up with possible solutions.

4. Filter by what you're most passionate about.

5. Narrow your ideas down to one.

Train Your Mind to Identify Areas of Opportunity:

Not every idea you come up with will be the million-dollar idea. The purpose is for you to start occupying your mind with ideas and the potential opportunities. The key to identifying the best topics is to identify the gaps in the market.

Start Making a List of Problem Solving

Now, you want to list all the problems associated with your ideas you listed in step 1. In this area, you will start building more opportunities that are associated with your ideas. In order to help solve the problems, you must do research and ask people who may consider the product that you may sell.

Come Up with Possible Solutions

By now, you should have plenty of problems listed and the next step is finding solutions to those problems. During this process, you may want to have someone you can fully trust to help you. An objective opinion is very helpful when coming up with a new business. During this phase, you can hit a brick wall trying to find a solution. No worries, just move on to the next idea. Consider a niche area of your product too. Instead of doing what everyone else is doing, you do the opposite so you can stand out. When you stand out, your product will sell better because you're offering something different from everyone else. Also during this phase, you want to expand related topics. You want to ensure that the solution you find does not exist already.

Filter by What You're Passionate About

Starting a successful business may take years. However, it's very important to find something that sparks a personal interest. A lack of interest is why a lot of people give up so fast when starting a business. They become overwhelmed with challenges and road blocks during the process. No entrepreneur is able to be 100% perfect and a top seller, but you know the areas you are an expert in and you'll be able to find people to help you with your weak areas.

I always love to talk about relationship issues with my friends and family. All of sudden, people start reaching out to me like I was an expert or something. I may not be an expert, but do a lot of educational reading on relationships. It was time to tell my story and help others. I have the story and knowledge but no experience in writing a book. So, in the area where I was weak, I hired someone to help me with the book process. This same rule applies to any genre of business.

Narrow Down Your Ideas

You now have a list of solutions to common problems that you are enthusiastic about pursuing. Now it's time to find out which business ideas will actually work. Your goal is to narrow down your list to just one idea is by testing out the market in a risk-free way. You want to find out if people would buy the product or service before spending any money into the business.

Your primary goal is to make money and be very successful at this stage. So please, pick something that can be very profitable long term. I see a lot of women selling the exact product that can easily fade away within the next 12 months. Your next business needs to generate income for you for at least the next 10 years or so.

It's Time to be your own BOSS - starting today!
Let's GO!

Chase Your Dream Career

In my previous section, we spoke about starting your own business. However, everyone does not have that entrepreneurial mind frame. There is nothing wrong with that either. I'm more so an entrepreneur but I do not mind working a full-time job either. In today's society, it's very hard to get that dream job you have always wanted. However, there are ways to get that $100K of your dream. When I finally landed my dream job at the YMCA, I had to put a lot of work in. First, I needed to change my thinking process of how to get HR's attention.

I hired a third-party company to review my resume, cover letter, and thank you letter. The company only created one resume that was geared towards one specific career. From that one resume, I was able to create multiple resumes for different positions I was interested in. Sometimes you have to invest into yourself to be successful. Next, I revamped my LinkedIn profile and start ed engaging more with my followers. I have close to 1,000 followers from different professional backgrounds and never took advantage of that platform.

To get more views on your resume, you can create an account with a company called Job Scan. They scan your resume against the job you applied for. If the scan is high that means that you're a good candidate for the job. I spent hours on that website until I hit the jackpot. Your search for your dream career can be very stressful- but never give up.

Another good way to land your dream career is to start attending networking events in your city. You'll be surprised who you may meet. We all have busy lives, but attend at least one networking event monthly. Also, join multiple job boards online and stay applying.

Letter to My Readers:

Side chicks may appear to be winning- but they don't have to. Don't feed them your man. Neither do you have to be a clueless side chick. Ask the questions and follow your gut if you feel something is not right.

My goal here is to provide insight through experience.

You should be the most important, most loved and most taken care of first. Self-evaluate you. Get out the slump. Dress well, look good, and feel great. Be good to yourself. Expand your social circle upward. Never settle for less and for liars. Don't forget to change it up and boss it up! If your instincts send up a yellow or red flag, check it out thoroughly. Don't lie to yourself. Be about your money, credit, health and education. Most importantly, acknowledge God and he will direct your path.

To my real side chick readers, the ones who know that's who you are, and that's who you want to be, I'm putting you on notice. I'm putting the word out to as many women as I possibly can. The fight is on. You ain't winning Shit.

–Shanti Helena

Social Media & Contact:
Instagram Info: shanti.helena
Email: contact@shantihelena.com
Website: www.shantihelena.com